Faith Devotional
for Teen Boys

BECOMING
WHO
I AM

ANDERS BENNETT

ADISAN Publishing AB

Introduction

Who are you? That can be a challenging question to answer if you think about it. Some days, it may feel like your answer to that question changes every hour. Sometimes you're a student, or sometimes you're an athlete. But underneath all of those things, there is something holding it all together. As you work your way through this study, I hope you will find that Jesus is the glue that is holding you together. It's like He is the foundation to your house. He is upholding all of who you are.

Throughout this book, we are going to look at how Jesus is the foundation of who you are affects everything about you. It changes how you are as a student or friend. It even changes how you handle your emotions or job opportunities. I trust this journey will be helpful as you are becoming who you are.

I AM in Christ

I Am Forgiven

"Be kind to one another, tenderhearted, forgiving one another, as God in Christ forgave you" - Ephesians 4:32

Who are you? I'm not asking your name or where you're from. I'm asking who you are as a person? What makes you, you? If you are a Christian, then the foundation of who you are is in Christ. Your very identity is rooted in who He is. Before we can discuss who you are, we have to know who He has made you to be.

In this verse, we can see that you are forgiven in Christ. This means that God has forgiven you for every failure in your life because of Jesus' sacrificial death on the cross. It's as if one of your teachers marked a test you failed with a passing grade. In abundant grace and mercy, the record has been set right for you. You are forgiven.

What is holding me back from forgiving others when I've been forgiven so much?

I AM in Christ

I Am Accepted

"Therefore welcome one another as Christ has welcomed you, for the glory of God." - Romans 15:7

Have you ever been somewhere new and felt entirely out of place? It may have felt as if you don't belong there. Maybe you've been somewhere new, but you were welcomed in by a friend. When that happens, the stresses of being in that new place begin to fade away.

In a much bigger way, we have been welcomed in by Jesus. In the presence of God, only those without any faults can stand. Since we all have our issues, the presence of God can be a terrifying place. Because of what Jesus has done for us, He has welcomed us into God's presence. There we can be at peace. In Christ, you are welcomed.

Whom can you welcome into your group of friends?

I Am a New Creation

"Therefore, if anyone is in Christ, he is a new creation. The old has passed away; behold, the new has come." - 2 Corinthians 5:17

If you are in Christ, you are a new person. This means that the way you live and the reasons you do what you do have changed. It may even mean that you have changed or ended friendships in order to follow Jesus. You're a new person, and that can be hard to be sometimes.

But being a new person is a great thing too. Being new means, you no longer live in the slavery of sin that you once did. It means that your new set of relationships are going to be life-giving and supportive. It means that you have a bigger purpose in life than pleasing certain people. Being made new can be difficult at times, but it is more than worth the effort.

Since following Jesus, what has been the most challenging change for you to make?

I AM in Christ

I Am Loved

"For God so loved the world, that he gave his only Son, that whoever believes in him should not perish but have eternal life." - John 3:16

You are loved. This is the message that everyone desperately wants and needs to hear. Think about it. One of the biggest fears we have in life is rejection. This is why it is so hard to ask someone on a date or to audition for a role in the school play. Being entirely yourself in front of others is scary because there is a chance they may turn away.

As Christians, we have a God who loves us so profoundly. He knows the horrible details of our sinful souls, and He still chooses to love us. He has not rejected us but has fully accepted us because of His Son, Jesus. We are known and loved by the Creator of all things.

When was the last time you were fearful of rejection?

I Am Protected

"My Father, who has given them to me, is greater than all, and no one is able to snatch them out of the Father's hand." - John 10:29

When you play sports, there's often some safety equipment that you have to wear. This is particularly important in sports like hockey or football. Without the helmets and pads, the hits you would take would be devastating. In dangerous games, you need protection in order to play without fear.

As followers of Jesus, we have protection in Christ. Read the promise that is given in our passage of scripture again. "No one is able to snatch them out of the Father's hand." No one! Not your worst enemy, your own failures, or the Devil can pluck you from the mighty hand of God. You are safe and sound in His grasp.

Why does protection provide confidence?

I Am Purified

*"Then they were each given a white robe and told to rest
a little longer, until the number of their fellow servants
and their brothers should be complete, who were to be
killed as they themselves had been." - Revelation 6:11*

The imagery of a white robe is symbolic in the book of Revelation. While it is entirely possible that we will wear white when we stand before our God in Heaven, what is meant by this verse is that we will be wearing righteousness. Because Jesus has paid the penalty for our sin, we can trade our filthy rags for garments that are as white as snow.

I want you to notice that these robes were given to them. They did not arrive with them. They did not pull them out of their closets for the big day. They were a gift. The same is true for you. God wants to give you the gift of His son. It's free, and there's no other way to receive it than to accept it from Him.

Have you accepted the free gift from God?

I AM in Christ

I Am Strong

*"Finally, be strong in the Lord and in the
strength of his might." - Ephesians 6:10*

Sports were really important to me growing up. It's where I made
friends, released some aggression, and learned to be a part of
a team. One of the sports I played was wrestling. In this sport,
there is a lot of emphasis on physical strength. We would spend
the same number of hours in the weight room as we would on
the wrestling mat. You had to be strong to compete well.

The same is true in Christian life. We must be strong to
compete well. Paul says that we are all running and race and
that we should strive to run with endurance. Praise be to God.
Our strength comes from Him to run this race. When the road
ahead is steep, and you're becoming weary, remember that you
are strong in Christ.

When do you feel the strongest?

I AM in Christ

I Am Justified

*"Therefore, since we have been justified
by faith, we have peace with God through
our Lord Jesus Christ." - Romans 5:1*

In Christ, we are justified. This may be a word you're not very familiar with. Let's be honest. It's not one that you use in everyday conversation. But it has an essential meaning that changes the way we view ourselves. A simple definition is when we are justified, it is "just as if I'd" never done it.

Where there was strife and difficulty, there is now peace. Perhaps you've experienced this with a friend that hurt you. If that friend made it up to you in a way that removed the hurt feelings, then they have been justified. The Bible teaches us that we have been justified before God because of the actions of Jesus. We can live in confidence and freedom because of it.

When have you had to justify yourself before someone else?

I AM in Christ

I Am Adopted

"he predestined us for adoption to himself as sons through Jesus Christ, according to the purpose of his will" - Ephesians 1:5

I had the privilege of adopting my son when he was four years old. Because of that experience, this verse means a lot to me. I know what it is like for a father to want a son who is not biologically his. I know the love that is there in the father's heart as he pursues a relationship with that son.

Friend, God the Father has adopted you into His family. He wants you. I don't know what your home life is like and what your relationship with your parents is. If it is strained, I hope you will find rest and encouragement in this truth about who you are in Christ: You are adopted by a Father who loves you so much He was willing to sacrifice His own Son to have you.

How does it feel to know that you are adopted by God?

I AM in Christ

I Am Complete

"And I am sure of this, that he who began a good work in you will bring it to completion at the day of Jesus Christ." - Philippians 1:6

You are becoming who You are. Who you are now is not who you will be in five or even fifty years? God is growing you and molding you into the image of His Son. He is the one who began changing you on the day you were saved, and He is the one who will continue to change you until you see Him face to face.

If there are areas in your life where you're struggling, don't give up. God's not done working on you. If there are strengths you have that you're tempted to boast about, remember the reason you have those strengths, to begin with. From this point on in our study, we are going to look at all the ways God is growing you while remembering where your identity lies: in Christ.

In what ways have you grown over the past year?

I AM Me

My Strengths

"All these are empowered by one and the same
Spirit, who apportions to each one individually
as he wills." - 1 Corinthians 12:11

We have all been created by the same God, but we are still different. We are all made with the same honor and value, but we have different strengths and giftings. Over the next ten devotions, we are going to take some time to think about the things that make you, you.

Let's first consider the strengths that God has given you. This does not have to be physical strength, but something that you're good at. Maybe you're good with numbers or good with people. It might be that you're athletic or that you're a reader. Whatever your strengths are, thank God for them. He has made you that way for a reason.

What strengths has God given you?

I AM Me

My Weaknesses

"All these are empowered by one and the same Spirit, who apportions to each one individually as he wills." - Romans 12:6

While we all have strengths, none of us are perfect. We all have weaknesses or areas we could grow in. This is important for us to realize about ourselves because it reminds us that we cannot do everything on our own. That truth points us back to Jesus, who offers to be with us and strengthen us each and every day.

It also helps to take the pressure off of us. Since we cannot be good at everything, we don't have to take the pressure of being the best. We can let go of those unrealistic expectations and accept help when we need it. Friend, it doesn't all ride on you. There are people ready and available to help. All we have to do is be humble and ask.

Why would God give you weaknesses?

I AM Me

My Personality

"Simon Peter said to him, "Lord, not my feet only but also my hands and my head!" - John 13:9

What is your personality like? I describe myself as an introvert who has learned to act like an extrovert. I prefer to be unseen and unheard by most people, but if I'm put in a social situation, I can meet whatever expectation there is. Peter, in our scripture today, is the kind of guy who speaks before he thinks. He is usually the first one to boldly stand up for someone, but he is also known for boldly ignorant statements.

When Peter said this, Jesus rebuked him because he had missed the point. Even though Peter's personality caused some issues along the way, God chose to use him as a critical person in the early church. Whatever personality you have, God can and wants to use you too.

How would you describe your personality?.

I AM Me

My Interests

"You turn things upside down! Shall the potter be regarded as the clay, that the thing made should say of its maker, "He did not make me"; or the thing formed say of him who formed it, "He has no understanding"?" - Isaiah 29:16

Your interests may be a key to finding out what God has planned for your life. God is a God of order and logic, so for Him to wire you to enjoy building things but then plan your life around paperwork wouldn't make the most sense. God loves to use people in unlikely situations, absolutely. But typically, God uses ordinary people doing ordinary things for an extraordinary God.

Look into that this week. Examine the things that interest you. Take a look at your hobbies and what you genuinely enjoy doing. Maybe God has a future for you in those things that will bring you joy and bring Him glory. I would also suggest trying new things and seeing what other interests you may have.

What do you like to do for fun?

I AM Me

My Design

"For you formed my inward parts; you knitted me together in my mother's womb." - Psalm 139:13

All of what we have been thinking about so far could be summarized into God's design for us. Think about it for a moment. Before your parents ever gave you a name, God had a clear design for you. Like an artist with a blank canvas, He saw you completely in His mind before He created you. He took time on you, and you are exactly as He wants you to be.

For some of us, it can be hard to embrace who we are because we would rather be someone else. Or at least have some of the qualities of someone else. I want to encourage you to embrace who you are, weaknesses and all. Embrace who God has designed you to be. No one can be a better you than you.

Do you struggle with how God has designed you?

I AM Me

His Image

"So God created man in his own image, in the image of God he created him; male and female he created them." - Genesis 1:27

Not only has God designed every detail of who you are, but He has also imprinted on you His very image. What does that mean? There are certain qualities about humanity that reflect the character of God. Think of yourself like a mirror or a photo. In a picture, you don't literally see yourself, just an image of yourself. That's how it is with us. There are ways in which we are like God but are not God.

Let's think about a few of the ways that we are like God. One of those ways is that we have a conscience. Go anywhere on the planet and steal from someone, and they will get mad. Why? Because everyone knows that stealing is wrong. It is written on our hearts. Another example is our creativity. We don't just build a shelter like other animals. We make it beautiful. God has imprinted on us His image. What an incredible thought.

How else are we like God?

I AM Me

His Plan

"which he will display at the proper time—he who is the blessed and only Sovereign, the King of kings and Lord of lords" - 1 Timothy 6:15

God has designed you and created you with a plan in mind. In fact, God has a plan for your life that is meant for your good and His glory. As our sovereign king, He reigns over everyone and everything. This puts Him in complete control of everything that happens to you.

God sometimes allows difficult things to happen to you. He does this for your ultimate good. In other words, it may not feel good now, and it may even be that someone has sinned against you. God will use those hard times to grow you and teach you how to trust Him more and more. Like sore muscles after a hard workout, the pain is real but temporary.

How does God's plan for you make you feel?

I AM Me

His Mission

"Go therefore and make disciples of all nations, baptizing them in the name of the Father and of the Son and of the Holy Spirit, teaching them to observe all that I have commanded you. And behold, I am with you always, to the end of the age." - Matthew 28:19-20

God's plan for your life includes a mission. The verse above is called the Great Commission. If you've trusted Jesus with your life, then this is the mission He has commissioned you on. He taught that we are to go and make disciples. What does that mean? It simply means that we are to teach people how to follow Jesus.

So where are we supposed to go? Does this mean that everyone needs to pack their bags and become an overseas missionary? No, but this does mean that every believer is a missionary. We are on a mission, at work, on the ball field, at work, and at home. Wherever we would naturally be going because of the rhythms of our lives, there we should be telling people about Jesus.

Where is your mission field?

I AM Me

My Gifts

"To each is given the manifestation of the Spirit for the common good". - 1 Corinthians 12:7

Unlike some of the natural talents that God has given you, He gives us spiritual gifts as well. There is not an exhaustive list of spiritual gifts in the Bible because the gift is less about the action and more about the result. For example, one spiritual gift might be teaching the Bible. This is a spiritual gift because it has a spiritual impact on someone's life. Another gift might be hospitality. Your welcoming kindness to others can do them spiritual good.

There are many different ways that you can do spiritual good to someone. You may be a good listener or great at giving advice. You might have incredible organizational skills that could help someone get their lives in order. Whatever you're good at, look into how you can do someone spiritual good with those giftings.

How can you help someone spiritually this week?

I AM Me

My Calling

*"For the gifts and the calling of God
are irrevocable." - Romans 11:29*

What are you going to do with your life? If you haven't had to answer this question yet, get ready. People are going to begin asking you questions like, "Where are you going to college?", "What kind of job are you going to get?" and "Where are you going to live?" When you think about these things, you're going to also have to consider what God has called you to do?

Here are two helpful things to help you figure that out. There is an inward calling and an outward calling. The inward calling is where you feel God pulling you in a particular direction. Like when you have peace after arriving on a college campus tour. The second is an outward calling. This is where trusted people in your life can affirm what you're thinking. If you want to be a lawyer, but all of your friends and family are saying otherwise, it might be time to reconsider what's best.

So, what are you going to do with your life?

I AM a Son

Honor Your Parents

"Honor your father and your mother, that your days may be long in the land that the Lord your God is giving you." - Exodus 20:12

If you're a teenage boy reading this book, that means that part of who you are is that you're a son. I don't know what your relationship is like between you and your father or your mother. It may be great, strained, toxic, or even non-existent. Whatever it may be, there is probably someone who is "parenting" you, even if it's not your biological parents.

Whomsoever that person is, the Bible teaches us to honor them. To honor someone means to show them respect in your actions and your attitude. When is the last time you honored your parents? A great way to do this is to simply tell them why you love them. You can make a list of reasons or just speak from the heart. Whatever it may be, honor your father and mother.

How can you honor your parents today?

Listen to Instruction

"Hear, my son, your father's instruction, and forsake not your mother's teaching," - Romans 15:7

"Are you listening to me?" If you're anything like me, then you've heard this question quite a bit. For me, it came when I was playing video games. I would be so wrapped up in what I was trying to accomplish on my game that I would block out everything and everyone else.

The Bible teaches us that we are supposed to listen to our parents. Specifically, we are supposed to take in their instructions and their teachings. This proverb is assuming that your parents are good and trustworthy. Most of us are blessed with those types of parents. If you are, listen to them. If you're not, do the work of filtering out what is ungodly and taking what is good.

When do you struggle to listen to your parents?

Learn from Discipline

"Know then in your heart that, as a man disciplines his son, the Lord your God disciplines you." - Deuteronomy 8:5

The purpose of discipline is not pain but discipleship. That's where we get that word. Discipline is supposed to be teaching us, not just stopping a behavior. When you're being disciplined, a good question to ask is, "What lesson do I need to learn from this?" Sometimes parents are really good at making that lesson clear.

Knowing that discipline is designed to teach and not to hurt should give us a new perspective on discipline. While discipline can be painful and frustrating, it will bring about some kind of good fruit in the end. The discipline that you experience is coming from a parent that loves you and wants the best for you.

What were you most recently disciplined for?

I AM a Son

Respect Your Parents

*"Whoever curses his father or his mother
shall be put to death." - Exodus 21:17*

Exodus 21:17 is a terrifying verse. Could our words lead to our death? Fear not because this was a part of the Mosaic Law for God's people in Israel. However, the heart of this command still resides in the Christian life. The root of this is respect for your father and mother. We are explicitly respecting them by not speaking poorly about them.

This doesn't mean you shouldn't vent to your friends about your life. Your parents are going to frustrate you, and you're going to frustrate them. What it does mean is that you shouldn't curse your parents. In other words, you should not wish for them to be hurt or killed out of anger or hatred. There should be a root of respect that keeps that fruit from coming forth.

Why did you get mad at your parents last?

Forgive Your Parents

"Fathers, do not provoke your children to anger, but bring them up in the discipline and instruction of the Lord." - Ephesians 6:4

I am a dad of two children. I have had to ask for forgiveness from both of them a handful of times in their lives. I want you to read this from a parent's heart for a moment. We make mistakes, and we need to be forgiven for those mistakes. Just like you, we're not perfect.

When your parents make a mistake or sin against you, talk with them about it. Express your hurt or your frustration. If they see and understand what they may have done to you, then they should ask for your forgiveness. When they do, forgive them. If they don't understand what they have done wrong and won't ask for forgiveness, then this gets much harder. However, in your heart, with God's help, you will still need to forgive them.

Have you ever had to forgive your parents?

I AM a Son

Trust Your Parents

"Train up a child in the way he should go; even when he is old he will not depart from it". - Proverbs 22:6

Have you ever thought about the fact that your parents used to be your age? Things that you're going through right now, it's possible that your parents have been through them. Struggles that are up ahead for you, your parents might know about a few of those as well. So, when the Proverbs tell your parents to train you up in the way you should 'go,' it's not guesswork.

It is a mixture of biblical advice and experience. With this in mind, I want to encourage you to trust your parents. If they say you need to stay away from certain friends or even certain girlfriends, trust them. If they think you can handle a bit extra school-wise, trust them. If they think you can't handle a job right now, trust them. They are speaking from experience. If they are Christians, they are speaking from biblical wisdom as well.

Have you ever lost trust in your parents?

I AM a Son

Obey Your Parents

*"Children, obey your parents in the Lord,
for this is right." - Ephesians 6:1*

There is very little wiggle room for us in this verse. However, it is not meant to be a straight jacket. This verse is assuming that all of what we are talking about is in place. This verse says that because your parents are honorable, trustworthy, imperfect, but respectable, they are worthy of being obeyed.

Obedience isn't the same thing as honor, but it is proof of it. Because you want to honor your parents, you obey them. Because you trust them, you do what they say. Because you respect them, you follow their directions. Let your obedience come from these foundations. Paul keeps it very simple in this verse to the Ephesian church. Obey your parents, for this is right.

Why have you disobeyed your parents in the past?

I AM a Son

Spiritual Father

"and what you have heard from me in the presence of many witnesses entrust to faithful men, who will be able to teach others also." - 2 Timothy 2:2

Everyone has a physical father, and if you're a believer, then you have a spiritual father as well. Your spiritual father is the person that is helping you to grow in your faith. Oftentimes, your physical and spiritual father are the same person. However, that's not always the case. While I lived with my father, it was my youth pastor who was my spiritual father. He helped me through a lot and taught me so much about Jesus.

If you're without someone like that in your life, I would put that at the top of your priority list. Whether it's your father, a pastor, or a good godly man that you know about, seek out a spiritual father. Find someone who will pour into your life and help you to grow spiritually. It will be one of the best relationships in your life.

Who is your spiritual father?

I AM a Son

Bless Your Parents

"Her children rise up and call her blessed; her husband also, and he praises her." - Proverbs 31:28

To bless someone means to say what is good and true about them. It has to be both of these things. If it is good but not true, then that person will know you're lying about them. If it's not good but true, then that can be hurtful and not a blessing. If you want to bless someone, you share with them something that is both good and true about them.

An example of this is that you may tell your mom that she is a great cook. Or you could tell your dad that you have learned a lot from him. Whatever it may be, take time to think about how you can bless your parents. What is something about them that is both good and true? Sharing this with them will be a huge encouragement and will strengthen your relationship.

How can you bless your parents?

I AM a Son

Be Honest with Your Parents

"And you will know the truth, and the truth will set you free." - John 8:32

In this last devotional regarding being a son, I'm going to challenge you with the most complex thing yet. Be honest with your parents. I'm not telling you to tell them every intimate detail of your life. You have things that you would like to keep private and personal. I understand that and your parents do too.

But if your parents ask you something that you feel like hiding, there's probably not a good reason for it. In fact, if your parents are asking, it's because they care. They may even know the answer to the question and just want to start the conversation with you. Hiding things is hard and painful. Be honest and let the truth set you free.

What is something you hide from your parents?

I AM a Friend

Faithful Friend

"Faithful are the wounds of a friend; profuse are the kisses of an enemy." - Proverbs 27:6

How can someone who wounds you be a friend? At first glance, this verse may not make a lot of sense. Let me put it into a different context. Which is more of a friend: someone who will tell you the truth, even if it hurts, or someone who lies to you? This is the idea behind this proverb. It is better to be told the truth by someone you trust than to be lied to by an enemy.

If you've ever watched a singing competition, then you've probably seen the results of "profuse kisses." Peoples' dreams are shattered when they find out that they aren't as good a singer as their mom or dad have told them they are. Be a faithful friend. Be willing to share the hard truths with those in your life.

When is the last time someone told you a hard truth?

I AM a Friend

Friends Lookout

*"He who withholds kindness from a friend forsakes
the fear of the Almighty." - Job 6:14*

Unfortunately, we are all guilty of withholding kindness from a
friend. Think about it. There has been a time in your life where
you were upset with one of your friends, and so you treated them
differently for a while. You walked past them without speaking,
you didn't sit with them around the lunch table, or you didn't
help them in a class because of some hurt.

Withholding that kindness is damaging to both your relationship with them and your relationship with God. When you
understand how much your sin has hurt God and He has not
withheld His kindness from you, that will overflow into your
friendships. When you've been hurt, go talk with them. Work it
out. Don't withhold your kindness for the sake of a grudge.

Have you been hurt by one of your friends recently?

I AM a Friend

Two Are Better Than One

"Two are better than one, because they have a good reward for their toil." - Ecclesiastes 4:9

We are all wired differently. Some of us love to be around people and feed of the energy in the room. Some of us are terrified of being in a large crowd and would rather be by ourselves. However, God has made you at a fundamental level. None of us want to be completely alone. We can't do this life alone.

This is why Solomon says that two are better than one. You can get more accomplished and do more complicated things when you work alongside someone. Working with someone has its own set of struggles, but the rewards are great, too. Who's that friend that has helped you? When you need a partner to get something done, who do you rely on?

What makes you an excellent partner to help others?

I AM a Friend

Friends Help

"For if they fall, one will lift up his fellow. But woe to him who is alone when he falls and has not another to lift him up!" - Ecclesiastes 4:10

After explaining that two are better than one, Solomon adds another reason why. He says that two are better than one because you have someone to support you. This may be a more important thing to realize when it comes to friendship. It's great to help someone accomplish something, but it is far more significant to be there for someone.

We are all going to fall in our lives. We may fall because of a problematic situation, a persistent sinful temptation, or an emotionally draining season. Whatever the reason is, you don't want to be alone when you fall. Not only do we need to find that friend that will be there to pick us up, but we also need to be that friend for someone else.

Who in your life needs to be picked back up?

I AM a Friend

Friends Encourage

"Therefore encourage one another and build one another up, just as you are doing." - 1 Thessalonians 5:11

One of the best experiences in life is when a trusted friend encourages you. When they offer those kind words, you can trust that they are trustworthy and that they are meant to lift you up. Encouragement, as this verse teaches, builds us. It picks us up when we are down and strengthens us when we are weak.

This is why encouragement is a mark of a true friend. A true friend wants to see you built up and wants to see you succeed in your endeavors. An authentic friend cheers for you when you get a higher rank on your sports team or band. A friend celebrates when you do well on a test even if they don't. Surround yourself with true friends.

Whom can you be an encouragement to today?

I AM a Friend

Friends are Good Company

"Do not be deceived: "Bad company ruins good morals." - 1 Corinthians 15:33

This verse starts off with "Do not be deceived," because far too often, people do not take this advice seriously. The truth is that whether we like it or not, we become like whom we hang out with. It rubs off on us. As the old saying goes, "If you lay down with dogs, you'll get fleas." It is essential for us to accept that we are not so strong and so independent that our friends won't change us.

This doesn't mean you cannot have friends of all kinds. But I would say that it cautions against having close friends whose lives you don't want to emulate. Think of how Jesus lived His life. He spent time with all kinds of people, but His close friends were His twelve disciples. Take time to consider who your inner circle of friends are and how they may be impacting your life?

Do you think you keep good or bad company?

Friends Forgive

"bearing with one another and, if one has a complaint against another, forgiving each other; as the Lord has forgiven you, so you also must forgive." - Colossians 3:13

When I was in middle school, one of my friends told a teacher that I threw a shoe at him. It was a ridiculous accusation and what made it worse is that I was punished for what I did not do. Needless to say, there was a stretch of time where I did not consider him to be my friend. After time and a challenging conversation, it came out that he genuinely thought I had done it.

This conversation changed my perspective and led me towards forgiveness. If I had genuinely thought someone did that to me, I might have reacted the same way. Whether you have had to yet or not, forgiveness is a necessary part of any friendship. You're going to offend them, and they are going to offend you. Be prepared to lean on the grace of God that was shown to be able to offer that to others.

Why is it difficult to forgive others?

I AM a Friend

Friends Are Close

"A man of many companions may come to ruin, but there is a friend who sticks closer than a brother." - Proverbs 18:24

I grew up in a family with two brothers. One was older than me by four years. We were pretty close and bonded over playing video games. My other brother is my twin. We bonded over almost everything because we experienced almost everything together. Even as close as I was with my brothers, this proverb was true for me. I had various friends at different points in my childhood who were closer than brothers.

The difference between a brother and a friend is that you get to choose your friend. You get to spend time with different people and decide who you want to let into your life. It's a beautiful privilege to be someone's friend because that means they have accepted you for who you are. Take time to thank God today for the friends He has put in your life.

Who are your friends that are closer than a brother?

I AM a Friend

Friends are Wise

"Whoever walks with the wise becomes wise, but the companion of fools will suffer harm" - Proverbs 13:20

Growing up, I had a friend that we called "Discovery." He was like a walking version of the Discovery Channel (a television station dedicated to learning about the world and wildlife). He seemed to know it all. I had another friend who struggled in school academically, but when it came to dealing with people and relationships, he was a genius. Which one of these guys is wise?

Trick question! Wisdom is not about knowledge or social skills. Wisdom is applied knowledge. If "Discovery" finds himself in the woods and has to survive, but does not use his knowledge, then he is not wise. Be a friend who not only has the knowledge but also uses it. Seek to be wise.

What makes someone wise?

I AM a Friend

Friends Love

"A friend loves at all times, and a brother is born for adversity." - Proverbs 17:17

The final mark of being a good friend is unconditional love. This type of friend does not leave you when you make a mistake. This type of friend does not act differently around you depending on who else is around. This type of friend keeps your secrets safe. These friends are, unfortunately, pretty rare. None of your friends will fulfill these things perfectly, but you will find some people who will stick around through thick and thin.

I want to challenge you today to be that friend. Be quick to listen, slow to speak, and slow to anger. Be forgiving and compassionate. Be trustworthy and honest. Be a friend who loves unconditionally. God will provide you the strength to do this because He has loved you in a greater way.

What does unconditional love mean to you?

I AM a Man

Men are Mature

"Until we all attain to the unity of the faith and of the knowledge of the Son of God, to mature manhood, to the measure of the stature of the fullness of Christ." - Ephesians 4:13

If you're reading this book, then you're becoming a man. In order to be the best man that you can be, you need to know what a man is. Over the subsequent ten sessions, we will take an overarching look at what it means to be a man biblically. The first thing we need to discuss is that men are mature.

Maturity means that you learn from your mistakes and you take responsibility for your actions. Spiritually speaking, it means that you're growing in your knowledge of God and your ability to follow Him faithfully. As you become a man, make these goals a top priority for you. Find ways to take on more responsibility and be faithful to keep your commitments.

On a scale of 1-10, how mature do others think you are?

Men Put Away Childish Things

"When I was a child, I spoke like a child, I thought like a child, I reasoned like a child. When I became a man, I gave up childish ways." - 1 Corinthians 13:11

Along with pursuing maturity, we have to put away childish things. Sometimes that's a pretty easy thing to do. Eventually, you're too big for a crib, and diapers aren't the most fashionable accessory to wear around. However, there are some childish ways that are more difficult to let go of. For example, becoming more independent and relying on yourself more than others can be hard.

You do not have to be an adult overnight (nor should you). You will need to start taking steps in that direction as you grow and mature into the man that God is calling you to be. We will discuss this more in a later devotion but think about finding a mentor to help you in that process.

What childish things are going to be difficult for you to let go of?

I AM a Man

Men Are Leaders

"But I want you to understand that the head of every man is Christ, the head of a wife is her husband, and the head of Christ is God." - 1 Corinthians 11:3

Men are called to be the spiritual leaders of their homes. You're probably not married or have children, but you can begin preparing yourself for this role and putting some of the principles into practice if you're dating. Being a spiritual leader means that you set the tone for spiritual health through example and encouragement.

If you're dating someone, you can bring up spiritual conversations and lead those discussions. It does not mean that you know everything or even know more than your partner. It does mean that you take the initiative to have those talks and lead towards healthy practices. This kind of leadership takes humility and intentionality. It takes work. Start thinking through how you might lead your family one day.

Do you consider yourself a spiritual leader? Why or why not?

47

I AM a Man

Men Keep Their Word

"Let what you say be simply 'Yes' or 'No'; anything more than this comes from evil." - Matthew 5:37

Mean what you say and say what you mean. That's the heart of this passage of scripture. This means that if you say that you're going to take out the trash, you take it out. It means that if you say you're not going to tell anyone about a friend's secret, then you don't talk. And it means that if you commit to a team or a group, then you're committed.

This also warns against ambiguous talk. I'm sure you've heard someone answer a question without really answering it. By saying a lot, they don't actually say anything at all. Let your answers be direct and honest. When you need to say no to something, just say no. You can give reasons if you feel like they are necessary, but no is enough sometimes too.

Do you have trouble telling people no?

I AM a Man

Men Bear Burdens

*"Bear one another's burdens, and so fulfill
the law of Christ." - Galatians 6:2*

You do not have to be a star athlete in order to bear someone's burdens. In fact, you don't even have to be able to run a mile to do the hard work of burden-bearing. All you need is time to listen and a compassionate heart. Bearing someone's burden is when you listen to the struggles of a friend and support them however you can.

It is called bearing burdens because when you hear what they are going through, you're going to feel the weight of it all. The beauty behind this is that when you begin to feel some of that weight, some of it gets lifted off of their shoulders. Together, you can bear much more than you can apart.

Whose burden can you lend a hand with?

I AM a Man

Men Confess Sin

"Therefore, confess your sins to one another and pray for one another, that you may be healed. The prayer of a righteous person has great power as it is working." - James 5:16

Confessing your sins to someone is one of the more difficult things that I am going to challenge you to do. In order to confess your sin, you have to identify it, accept it, take ownership of your actions, and then be humble and honest as you tell someone you trust about it. It takes a lot of work to confess your sin.

And you shouldn't confess your sins to just anybody. It takes a strong relationship of trust and vulnerability to be able to bear that weight. But when that relationship is in place, and you have someone you can confess to, you'll find freedom in that confession. You'll also find accountability for your actions because your friend will know what you're struggling with.

Why is it difficult for us to confess our sins to someone?

I AM a Man

Men Fight Temptation

"Submit yourselves therefore to God. Resist the Devil, and he will flee from you." - James 4:7

Temptation is all around you. If you have a smartphone, then you have access to all kinds of sinful sites and soul-damaging links. I wish I could say that as you get older, the fight gets more manageable. Unfortunately, that's not the case. The fight changes, and some seasons are easier than others, but temptation will always play a part in your life.

So, how do you fight it? How do you stand up against so strong an enemy? The answer is found in this verse. The first thing is to submit to God. Give your life entirely over to Him and trust Him to provide the strength you need. The second thing follows suit. Take that confidence and strength given to you by God and run. Run hard. Run from the Devil and the temptations he puts in your path.

What temptation do you struggle with the most?

I AM a Man

Men Are Gentle and Lowly

"Take my yoke upon you, and learn from me,
for I am gentle and lowly in heart, and you will
find rest for your souls." - Matthew 11:29

I don't know about you, but when I think of manliness, the terms gentle and lowly do not come to mind. These are the very words that Jesus used to describe Himself. If that is the type of man Jesus is, then that is the type of man we ought to strive to be as well.

What does a gentle and lowly man look like? He boldly defends others while holding his tongue when personally attacked. He confronts in a manner of love that assumes the best of others. He is someone you can trust to keep you physically, emotionally, and spiritually safe. With all of our hearts, let's strive to be like our Savior.

In what ways are you gentle and lowly?

Men Are Bold

"But Peter, standing with the eleven, lifted up his voice and addressed them: "Men of Judea and all who dwell in Jerusalem, let this be known to you, and give ear to my words." - Acts 2:14

In this passage from the Bible, Peter boldly preaches to a large crowd of people. The boldness is not in his ability to stand before a crowd and deliver a message but in the brutal truth in the message. He was about to proclaim that Jesus was the only way to be saved and that the Jewish people in the crowd were responsible for His death.

These were hard words to hear and even harder to say. It took a boldness in the truth of his message for him to be able to share it. We, too, can speak boldly in the truth of our message. We don't have to shrink back in fear when someone confronts us about what we believe. We know that it's true, even if we cannot fully explain it.

How does knowing the truth make you a bold person?

I AM a Man

Men Stand Up for Others

"Open your mouth for the mute, for the rights of all who are destitute." - Proverbs 31:8

We live in a world that isn't always just. This means that people are mistreated. This may be because of the color of their skin, where they were born, their gender, or even their age. Because the world is filled with sinful people that think about themselves first, we can twist the uniqueness of others and turn them into faults.

When Solomon writes in Proverbs for us to speak up for the rights of those who are destitute, he is telling us to put others before ourselves. He is encouraging us to see our differences as beautiful colors in God's grand design. Some people cannot speak up for themselves, and when we find them, we should. If you see someone being mistreated, don't assume that they can defend themselves. Step in and speak up.

How does speaking up for someone encourage them?

I AM in Trouble

God Can Save

"This poor man cried, and the Lord heard him and saved him out of all his troubles." - Psalm 34:6

Inevitably in your life, you're going to find yourself in trouble. We all make mistakes that put us in difficult situations. Sometimes we're in trouble, and it's not our fault. Whatever the reason is, we have a God who wants us to cry out to him when we are in trouble.

My son, when he gets sick or scared at night, he does not lay there in silence. He doesn't try to tough it out and go through it alone. He calls out for help. He is not supposed to handle those things alone. Friend, you are not supposed to handle your trouble alone. You have a good God who hears you when you call and responds with love and mercy.

Are you in trouble now? If so, what's going on?

I AM in Trouble

Take Refuge

"The Lord is good, a stronghold in the day of trouble; he knows those who take refuge in him." - Nahum 1:7

In wartime scenarios, everything is heightened. Your senses are on full alert, picking up every possible intrusion. This causes things like fear or anxiety to take hold of our souls and keep us captive. But even in those situations, there are moments of rest. There are foxholes or bunkers to duck down in. There are fellow soldiers that are watching over you as you sleep. There are moments of refuge.

In our verse today, we read that we can take refuge in our God. Our God is not like a bunker or foxhole that only provides temporary cover. He is not like a fellow soldier watching over us who is prone to mistakes or falling asleep himself. No, our God is powerful and safe. He is our only true refuge in this life.

Where do you go to find refuge?

I AM in Trouble

Wait for the Lord

"Wait for the Lord; be strong, and let your heart take courage; wait for the Lord!" - Psalm 27:14

Patience is not my strong suit. Sometimes I struggle to wait on the microwave to finish heating up my breakfast. When the bible says to wait for the Lord, it feels like an impossible task. Even now, as I write this devotional, I have to wait on the Lord for clarity on a few things in my life. Waiting is hard.

Let's take a moment to consider why waiting on the Lord is the best thing we can do. First, the Lord is always on time. We don't wait because He is late or because His plans are falling through. They are right on schedule. Second, we wait because God knows what is best for us. Whatever is coming and whatever time it comes is what will be for our good, His glory. So, join with me and wait for the Lord.

What are you waiting for to happen?

I AM in Trouble

God Hears You

"Before they call, I will answer; while they are yet speaking, I will hear." - Isaiah 65:24

Every time I think about it, this truth astonishes me to the core. God listens to us. I cannot fathom this because He is a busy and holy God. He has other things to concern Himself with, like upholding all of creation. And yet, there is such a love in Him that bends His ear to listen to rebellious sinners like us.

Notice, though, what is written in Isaiah. Before we even call out, God has the answer. While we are still speaking, God has already heard. He knows the depths of our hearts and what we need far before we say a word about it. He stands ready to listen and respond at the right time. We can confidently bow before His throne and find mercy and justice every time.

How does God listening to you make you feel?

I AM in Trouble

Overcome

"I have said these things to you, that in me you may have peace. In the world you will have tribulation. But take heart; I have overcome the world." - John 16:33

In this verse, Jesus promises us two things. The first promise is that in this world, we will have tribulation. We know this is true because we have all faced complex circumstances. Some of us have faced more difficult challenges in our lives than others. But the truth remains that tribulation comes for all of us at some point in our lives. However, that's not the only promise He made.

He said to take heart because he has overcome the world. This means that no matter the difficulty that you're facing in your life, Jesus has already overcome that. There is no problem that is too difficult for Him. There is no tribulation that will stop Him or make Him think twice. If He can overcome death and the grave, what else could possibly stand in His way?

What problem do you need to trust Jesus to handle?

I AM in Trouble

A Very Present Help

"God is our refuge and strength, a very present help in trouble." - Psalm 46:1

We have already read about how God is a perfect and robust refuge, but the psalmist here makes a further point. He is present. Have you ever been or felt alone when trouble came? Have you wondered what to do or where to turn to? The Bible says that God Himself is a very present help in our troubles.

Like the air that we breathe or the blood coursing through our veins, He is always there, and He is keeping us alive. There is a sense in which He is like a smartphone. He is by your side and full of answers. The issue we often face is we would instead go to our smartphone than to our God when trouble arises.

What does God's presence mean to you?

Hold Fast

"so that by two unchangeable things, in which it is impossible for God to lie, we who have fled for refuge might have strong encouragement to hold fast to the hope set before us." - Hebrews 6:18

One of the things that I learned while playing football in high school was how to hold a football when being tackled. While you're running, holding the ball in one arm off to the side would allow you to run faster. However, if you were about to get hit, you had to wrap the ball up with both arms and protect it. You had to hold fast to the ball and refuse to let go.

In this passage from Hebrews, we are told to hold fast to the hope that is set before us. There will be plenty of things trying to tackle us in our lives. There will be peer pressure from friends, grades that have to be kept up, and work to be done on time. Through it all, we must hold fast to our hope in Jesus.

How can we hold fast to hope?

I AM in Trouble

God is With You

"fear not, for I am with you; be not dismayed, for I am your God; I will strengthen you, I will help you, I will uphold you with my righteous right hand."- Isaiah 41:10

God is with you. This promise is seen all over the Bible. The Father promises that He will never leave nor forsake His people. Jesus, the Son, says in His great commission that He will be with us always, even to the end of the age. The Holy Spirit, in the most intimate way, dwells within us and will not leave us. God is with us.

Notice what the presence of God brings. He brings courage, strength, help, righteousness, and someone to uphold us. In short, He brings with Him all that we need in life to face any circumstance. God's presence with us is not like an old receipt but like a map. He is helpful to tackle the challenges of the day.

What do you do when you feel like God is not with you?

He Goes Before You

"Then I said to you, 'Do not be in dread or afraid of them. The Lord your God who goes before you will himself fight for you, just as he did for you in Egypt before your eyes" - Deuteronomy 1:29-30

Our God is so powerful that not only can He promise to be with us always, but He can also promise to go before us. Our God is omnipresent, which means that He is at all places at all times. This is hard for us to fully grasp because nothing else in all of creation is like that, not even oxygen. But because He is, He can both be with us and go before us.

With that powerful of a God going before us, what do we have to fear? Like in football, the running back has nothing to fear with a solid offensive line blocking the other team. Someone bigger and stronger than him is leading the way. The same is true for us as we follow our God.

What benefit is there for us if God goes before us?

I AM in Trouble

Delight in His Word

"Trouble and anguish have found me out, but your commandments are my delight." - Psalm 119:143

As we finish this section on how to handle troubles in your life, my final encouragement would be for you to delight in God's word. Begin or end your day (depending on if you're a morning person or not) with the word of God speaking to and comforting your soul. You'll be truly amazed at how daily soul care like that will put your troubles into perspective and even give wisdom on how to handle them.

If you're doing this devotional, then you're already building that habit into your daily routine. I would encourage you to take it one step further. Read a chapter a day from the Bible and work your way through the different books. Start in the New Testament with one of the gospels (Matthew, Mark, Luke, or John) and go from there.

What did you learn from God's word that encouraged you?

I AM Confused

God of Peace

"For God is not a God of confusion but of peace."
- 1 Corinthians 14:33

Let's face it; sometimes, we get confused. The confusion I want to talk about is not like you're confused about a math problem. The confusion I want to focus on is the one that leads to anxiety and fear. It's when you've got a big decision to make, and you don't know what to do. It's when your friends are giving you the cold shoulder, and you don't know what's wrong. That's the kind of confusion that we will take a look at over the following few devotions.

As we walk with Jesus, we must trust the fact that God is a God of peace and not confusion. So, when we're feeling anxious or stressed because we don't know what to do, that's not God's design. However, His answer is not always to make it clear what we should do. Oftentimes, He simply wants us to trust Him for a while.

When was the last time your confusion led to fear?

I AM Confused

Understanding

"Think over what I say, for the Lord will give you understanding in everything." - 2 Timothy 2:7

What do you do when you don't understand something in school? You read your textbook for more information. You ask your teacher for clarification. You talk to your friends or your parents about it and get some help from them. If you are confused about something, you go to someone for help. The same ought to be true in your walk with Jesus.

The fantastic thing about our God is that He has given us a textbook. He Himself is our great Teacher. He has given us brothers and sisters in the faith, even spiritual parents, to help us along the way. When you're not sure what to do next or how to handle something, dig into the resources that God has provided for. He will give you understanding.

In what area of your life do you lack understanding?

Ask God for Wisdom

"If any of you lacks wisdom, let him ask God,
who gives generously to all without reproach,
and it will be given him." - James 1:5

While understanding is a vital part of growing as a believer, wisdom is the next step. Wisdom is applied understanding. For example, understanding is knowing what a basketball is and how to take a shot. Wisdom is getting yourself into a position to give yourself the best chance at making the shot. Wisdom oftentimes comes through experience. However, God promises to give wisdom to us if we ask for it.

This means that we don't necessarily have to learn "the hard way" in order to have wisdom. We can ask God without fear and trust that He will provide it. He does this in similar ways to how He provides understanding. A key to this is knowing that someone in your life has probably already been through what you're going through, and God has placed them in your life to give you wisdom.

Who is someone in your life that is wise?

Be Sober-Minded

*"Be sober-minded; be watchful. Your adversary
the devil prowls around like a roaring lion,
seeking someone to devour." - 1 Peter 5:8*

Be sober-minded. This is a call to us to think clearly about what's going on around us and in us. This does not mean that we have to have everything figured out or even understand all that is going on around us. Essentially, we need to be able to filter everything that is going on through the Word of God for our understanding.

When someone in your life is in a car accident, it's natural to freak out for a moment. It's common to lose your sober-minded state because of all of the questions and concerns that come flooding in. The way to remain sober-minded in those moments is to quickly run back to what you know for sure. You know that God is good, and He loves His people. You know that we live in a broken world, and bad things happen. You know that God will be with you and the individuals in the accident. These things sober your mind.

*What verse of scripture can you run
to for comfort in difficult times?*

I AM Confused

Spirit of Truth

" When the Spirit of truth comes, he will guide you into all the truth, for he will not speak on his own authority, but whatever he hears he will speak, and he will declare to you the things that are to come." - John 16:13

One of the names that our God goes by is the Spirit of Truth. This should be a massive comfort for us. He holds within Himself all that is true. For any question, He has the answer. All truth that we find in the world today, whether from the Bible or in a science book, is ultimately from God. He is the Spirit of truth.

And He promises to guide us in all truth and show us the things that are to come. He isn't an angry librarian holding the keys to the building. He openly shares His knowledge and wisdom with us at the right time. He wants us to grow and succeed. This is why we can lean on Him and go to Him for help in our times of need.

What picture comes to mind when you hear "Spirit of Truth?"

I AM Confused

Not Driven to Despair

"We are afflicted in every way, but not crushed; perplexed, but not driven to despair;" - 2 Corinthians 4:8

Paul was a missionary in the early church. He faced incredible hardship in his life. He was imprisoned multiple times, endured shipwreck, and much more. So for him to encourage the Corinthian church to be afflicted and perplexed, but not crushed or in despair, it is significant. He knew what it meant to be afflicted more than most of us.

How is it he would avoid being crushed or in despair? The answer is simple: He trusted Jesus. He knew that God loved him so much that He sent His Son to die for him. If God would not spare His own Son to provide for His people, why would we be drawn to despair? How could we possibly be crushed? Be encouraged, and do not despair. Jesus loves you.

What is the hardest thing you've had to endure?

I AM Confused

The Heart

"The heart is deceitful above all things, and desperately sick; who can understand it?" - Jeremiah 17:9

One of the most helpful verses in understanding the effects of our sin is written above. It teaches that our hearts are not to be trusted. This is contrary to what the world loves to tell us. Almost every children's movie out there teaches us to follow our hearts or trust our guts. The issue with that is our heart is deceitful and sick. This is why we desperately need Jesus,

    We need Him to change our hearts. Better yet, we need Him to give us a spiritual heart transplant. We need Him to take residence in our souls and guide us each day. I urge you, friend, don't follow your heart. Follow Jesus. He is a far better and more trustworthy leader.

What does it mean to follow your heart?

I AM Confused

Trust in the Lord

"Trust in the Lord with all your heart, and do not lean on your own understanding. In all your ways acknowledge him, and he will make straight your paths." - Proverbs 3:5-6

When I was a kid, during the summer school break, my dad would always have a list of chores for us to do each day. It didn't matter when we did them as long as they were done before he got home at dinner time. My brother and I would fight over who got to do what chores. Nobody wanted to weed eat! One day, dad left a chore that we all had to do. It was to memorize Proverbs 3:5-6.

I didn't understand why he wanted us to do that then, but I am so thankful now. This verse has helped me countless times in my life. As you get older, you're going to be faced with life-altering decisions like where to go to school, what job to pursue, or whom to marry. Trust in the Lord with all your heart. Commit this verse to memory.

Instead of a question this time, take time to commit this verse to memory.

I AM Confused

Spirit of Power

"for God gave us a spirit not of fear but of power and love and self-control." - 2 Timothy 1:7

What spirit is reigning in you? This may be a question you have never considered before. Paul tells Timothy that there is a spirit of fear that is lurking around, seeking to gain control of our souls. But God has not given us that spirit. The enemy comes in with the spirit of fear. Our God has given us a spirit of power, love, and self-control.

Let me ask the same question in another way. What is at the core of your heart? What is driving you? Is it fear? Or are you driven by the power of God, the love of God, and the self-control that only God can provide? Let the Spirit of God have His way in your heart. Let Him take control.

What spirit is reigning in you?

I AM Confused

He Cares for You

"Casting all your anxieties on him, because he cares for you."- 1 Peter 5:7

When faced with confusion that leads to fear and anxiety, Peter provides us with a clear direction. He tells us to cast our anxieties on God because He cares for us. How do you do that? How do you cast anxiety on someone? It's not like it is something you can put into a box and toss in the back of your truck.

We cast our cares by trusting God with them. When we bow to Him in prayer and confess our inability to handle the situation, and ask God to take charge, that's when we cast them on Him. And He is happy to take our worries for two reasons. The first is that He loves us and wants to help us. The second is that what worries us doesn't cause Him an ounce of fear. He can take whatever you have to throw at Him.

Why are you anxious today?

Be Angry

"Be angry and do not sin;" - Ephesians 4:26

For many of us, this feels like a contradiction. We often associate anger with sin. And to be fair, most of the time, when we get angry, it's either for a sinful reason, or we do something sinful in our anger. However, Paul is telling the Ephesian church that there is a way to be angry and not sin. What is that way?

He is talking about righteous anger. For example, if you hear about someone who is being bullied, that ought to make you mad. If you're mistreated, anger is the correct emotional response. When you study history and see all the reasons wars have been started, it's supposed to make you angry. You can be angry over sinful things. The challenge for us is how to handle that anger. Over the next few devotionals, we will see what the Bible has to say about it all.

What was the last thing to make you angry?

I AM Angry

Don't Let the Sun Go Down

"Do not let the sun go down on your anger," - Ephesians 2:26

Right after saying, "Be angry and do not sin," Paul continues to tell us how. He says that the first thing we need to do is handle our emotions. The first thing is not to react. When you've been maltreated, the first step is not to lash out. The first step is to process that anger and calm back down.

This may take some time in order to accomplish, but Paul says to not let the sun go down on your anger. This doesn't mean you don't go to sleep mad. This means don't ignore your anger and soak in your anger, and act likes it's not there. Don't continue in your day like nothing is wrong, and go to sleep. By reflecting on God's word and getting advice from friends, process your anger with someone.

Why should you not ignore your feelings of anger?

I AM Angry

Jesus' Anger

"And Jesus entered the temple and drove out all who sold and bought in the temple, and he overturned the tables of the money-changers and the seats of those who sold pigeons." - Matthew 21:12

Jesus got angry. Did you realize this? When He entered the temple, Jesus got so angry at what He saw that the Bible says He flipped the tables over. Elsewhere it says He made a whip and drove the people out. How could Jesus do these things and not sin? Where is the righteousness behind this anger?

Jesus is God. So, when He walked into His temple and found people being taken advantage of and illegitimate sacrifices being offered to Him, the wrath of God was welling up inside of Him. Only Jesus could have acted this way and not sinned because only God was being sinned against in such a despicable way.

How does the fact that Jesus got angry change how you view anger?

I AM Angry

Unwarranted Anger

*"But for Cain and his offering, he had no regard.
So Cain was very angry, and his face fell." - Genesis 4:5*

The story of Cain and Abel is the first story that we come across after Adam and Eve are kicked out of the Garden in the beginning. Cain and Abel are their sons. In this story, we learn about how God accepted Abel's sacrifice to him, but not Cain's. As we study, we find that God accepted Abel's sacrifice because it was the best he had to offer and was given with pure motives. The same could not be said for Cain.

So, when Cain's sacrifice was rejected, he got angry. This is unwarranted anger. It was anger that was rooted in not getting his way. Cain got mad because he broke the rules and got in trouble for it. Have you been there before? You're upset that it turned out how you expected but not how you wanted. That's childish and unwarranted anger. Flee from that type of thinking.

When is the last time your anger was childish?

I AM Angry

Uncontrolled Anger

"Cain spoke to Abel, his brother. And when they were in the field, Cain rose up against his brother Abel and killed him." - Genesis 4:8

As the story continues, Cain becomes so angry with the situation. He kills Abel. This uncontrolled anger led to the first murder in human history. Remember, this all happened because of Cain's childish anger. It grew and festered and became a monstrous problem.

The same can happen when we harbor anger. When we let it settle in like an old stain, it lingers and grows and becomes uncontrolled. The foolishness of all of this is made more apparent when we remember that Cain wasn't angry at Abel, to begin with. He was angry with God for not accepting the sacrifice and himself for getting caught. Abel just received the uncontrolled anger from his brother. Don't allow your anger to go unchecked and uncontrolled.

When was the last time you lost control of your anger?

Righteousness of God

"For the anger of man does not produce the righteousness of God." - James 1:20

Anything done out of anger alone will not produce the righteousness of God. Think about Jesus' anger when He saw what was being done in the temple. On the surface, we just see His anger. But when you read the Bible and understand more about who He is and why He does what He does, you'll see that the anger is not alone. There is great compassion for the people who were being treated poorly. There was zeal for the holiness of God. It was not just anger.

Not only that, but He didn't let it end in personal anger. His anger, with other motivations, led Him to action. What makes you righteously angry? Is it bullying? Unfair treatment of others? Favoritism? Racism? Whatever it is, don't just be angry. Do something about it. Stand up for those who can't, out of compassion for them.

What other emotions direct your anger?

I AM Angry

Soft Answers

"A soft answer turns away wrath, but a harsh word stirs up anger." - Proverbs 15:1

Let's change the scenario for this one. We've been thinking about what to do when we are angry. Now, let's think about how to handle someone else who is angry. The proverb says that we should use a soft answer to someone who is angry. Otherwise, we will further their anger. What does that look like?

Imagine your dad is upset with you because you did not clean up your room. Which response will turn away his wrath and lead towards reconciliation? Would it be you lashing back at him with a loud voice? Or would it be you calmly explaining why you hadn't done that yet? The soft answer brings the intensity of the situation down. It allows everyone to hear each other and come to the best conclusion.

When someone is angry with you, do you tend to lash back?

I AM Angry

Slow to Anger

"Know this, my beloved brothers: let every person be quick to hear, slow to speak, slow to anger;" - James 1:19

Let this be a verse that you commit to memory. It will help you in a variety of ways and lead you towards a more Christ-like life. It is one that is simple to memorize but difficult to follow. Not many of us are quick to hear. Think about it. Most of the time, when someone is talking to us, we're thinking about what to say in response instead of truly listening.

This only leads us towards speaking too quickly. We like to offer up a response or a solution when all our friends need is just to be heard. Let them vent their frustrations. But don't grow angry with them. Be slow to anger so that when the time comes, you'll be ready to speak wise and helpful words. Write this verse down and put it somewhere you can see it every day for the next week.

Are you a good listener?

I AM Angry

Anger's Home

"Be not quick in your spirit to become angry, for anger lodges in the heart of fools." - Ecclesiastes 7:9

This verse is illuminating for us as we think about how anger works in our lives. It says that anger lodges in our hearts. It doesn't hang out in our front yards. It doesn't pitch and tent and camp in our backyard. No, it moves in. It grabs a bed and puts its close in the closet. It settles in for the night.

A heart like this is dangerous. There is only one throne for your soul, and it ought to be occupied by the Holy Spirit. The One who brings about love, joy, peace, patience, kindness, gentleness, and self-control. But when anger moves it, it fights for the throne too. Brother, do not be quick to become angry because it will be quick to keep you angry.

How does that imagery change how you view anger?

I AM Angry

Punishment for Anger

"But I say to you that everyone who is angry with his brother will be liable to judgment; whoever insults his brother will be liable to the council; and whoever says, 'You fool!' will be liable to the hell of fire." - Matthew 5:22

Your anger doesn't just hurt people's feelings. It does more damage than straining your relationships with others. It brings about more punishment than being disciplined by a parent, teacher, or boss. The punishment for anger is the same as for any other sin. When we lash out in anger, we bring about the wrath of God.

This is why we must trust in Jesus for everything in our lives, even our emotions. As we have seen, Jesus was angry but never sinned in His anger. Because He was able to do that perfectly for us, we can be seen as right before God. The Bible says that if we believe in Jesus' perfect life, sacrificial death, and victorious resurrection, then we will be given His right standing before the Father. Lean on Jesus and what He has done for you.

What else do you remember Jesus getting righteously angry about?

84

I AM Jealous

Jealousy Causes Disorder

"For where jealousy and selfish ambition exist, there will be disorder and every vile practice." - James 3:16

Like anger, jealousy is another emotion that will wreak havoc on your life. Also, like anger, it's an emotion that you will feel for the rest of your life. When your friends get nicer clothes or a car before you do. Or when you're the only one who doesn't have a girlfriend. Or when you see that some of your friends always do better than you in school, jealousy will rear its ugly head.

Over the next few devotions, we will see how jealousy brings about the disorder that James talks about in this verse. It messes everything up and puts our perspectives in the wrong order. It will cause us to think of ourselves as more important than anyone else, even Jesus Himself.

What makes you jealous?

I AM Jealous

Quarrels

"You desire and do not have, so you murder. You covet and cannot obtain, so you fight and quarrel. You do not have, because you do not ask. You ask and do not receive, because you ask wrongly, to spend it on your passions." - James 4:2-3

As you may notice, James has had a lot to say about both anger and jealousy. If you've never really read the book of James, I would encourage you to do that soon. Take it a chapter at a time. He is very understandable and practical in how he writes. Here he explains the heinous outcome of our jealousy.

He says plainly that when we desire but do not get what we want, then we murder. Now, it's not as quick as that, but it is as simple as that. When we allow jealousy to take root in our hearts, we will stop at nothing to get what we want. If you'll notice, one of the roots of anger is jealousy. So, if you're angry, think about what you might be jealous of.

When was the last time you were jealous?

I AM Jealous

Rotting the Bones

"A tranquil heart gives life to the flesh, but envy makes the bones rot." - Proverbs 14:30

If anger takes up residence in our hearts, then jealousy rots our bones to their core. I want you to hear how debilitating that is. Rotting bones break and infect the body. They're a ticking time-bomb to the destruction of the body. Jealousy has this kind of damaging effect on your soul. It is a ticking time-bomb.

It will start off small, and you'll keep it to yourself. The longer you do, the more it will grow. It will spread like cancer in your bones until it is all you can think about. Soon, you'll be just moments away from some of the drastic actions that you thought you would never do. When you're feeling jealous, confess that to God and to whoever is involved.

Why is it hard to confess jealousy?

I AM Jealous

Crushing Weight

"Wrath is cruel, anger is overwhelming, but who can stand before jealousy?" - Proverbs 27:4

Once again, we see the Bible connecting anger and jealousy. Notice how it talks about these topics this time. It calls wrath cruel and anger overwhelming. However, it seems to take it a step further with jealousy. It asks the question of who can even stand before jealousy. It is so overwhelming and crushing that men cannot stand before it.

If you've been jealous of someone's athletic ability for a long time, then you've felt this happen. Instead of being able to say good job, jealousy weighs in to keep you silent or snide. Instead of encouraging your friend to continue to grow, jealousy squeezes you to think evil thoughts to yourself or share them with a friend. Beware of the crushing weight of jealousy.

Who have you been jealous of lately?

I AM Jealous

Will Not Inherit

"envy, drunkenness, orgies, and things like these. I warn you, as I warned you before, that those who do such things will not inherit the kingdom of God." - Galatians 5:21

Once again, we see the Bible bringing the ultimate weight to bear on us. Jealousy or envy is on the list of sins that will keep us from the kingdom of God. You may not have dealt with drunkenness, but you have undoubtedly been jealous. This means that you are not worthy of being a part of God's kingdom.

But praise God. He knows this and has fixed the problem. He sent His Son, Jesus, to live a life without any hint of jealousy. Although He did not deserve it, He died on the cross. There He took our punishment. If we believe in what He has done for us, then we are transferred from the kingdom of darkness to the kingdom of God.

Have you ever thought about how Jesus is the answer to all of our sin issues?

I AM Jealous

Loveless

"love does not envy or boast;" - 1 Corinthians 13:4

1 Corinthians 13 is a section of Scripture that is often read at a wedding. In this chapter, Paul defines love in a beautiful way. We're taking just a part of that definition to understand something about jealousy or envy. Paul makes it clear that love does not envy. In other words, it is not loving to be jealous.

Whether you're jealous of someone's things, their personality, or who they are as a person, you cannot love them and be jealous of them. Take that idea and put it into a dating relationship. Jealousy will kill your relationship. We justify our jealousy by saying we really care about that person, but the opposite is true. We care about ourselves and are seeking to keep ourselves from getting hurt. Love does not envy.

Why is love not jealous?

I AM Jealous

Contentment Cure

"I know how to be brought low, and I know how to abound. In any and every circumstance, I have learned the secret of facing plenty and hunger, abundance and need." - Philippians 4:12

In light of all that we have learned about jealousy, let's take a moment to consider what the cure is. How do we fight the disease of envy? Paul teaches us in the book of Ephesians about the contentment cure. Paul learned how to live in complete contentment because, at different points in his life, he was either wealthy or poor. He learned how to be happy in any of the circumstances he found himself in.

This contentment resists jealousy because jealous comes along when you're not content. Instead of taking time to think about what you wish you had or how you wish you were, thank God for what you do have and who you are. This contentment will slowly provide the antidote to the jealousy that has been coursing through your veins.

What is your definition of contentment?

I AM Jealous

Fiercest as The Grave

"Set me as a seal upon your heart, as a seal upon your arm, for love is strong as death, jealousy is fierce as the grave. Its flashes are flashes of fire, the very flame of the Lord." - Song of Solomon 8:6

The song of Solomon is a love song between two people who want to be with each other. In this passage, their love for each other is described as strong and death, and their jealousy for each other as fierce as the grave. Maybe you read that, and a red flag went off in your mind. Isn't jealousy sinful? Not all of the time.

Like with anger, jealousy can be righteous. Our God is described as a jealous God. What does righteous jealousy look like? Righteous jealousy is rooted in love. When the songwriter says that their jealousy is as fierce as the grave, it is only after they have said it is as strong as death. They love the other person so much that all they want is their love in return. At its core, that is a good thing. However, we often twist it to be self-serving and protective.

How can God be jealous?

I AM Jealous

Steals Joy

"But he was angry and refused to go in. His father came out and entreated him" - Luke 15:28

In the story of the Prodigal Son, we hear about a younger son who wants his inheritance now, before his father passes away. He takes that money and wastes it all on wild living and finds himself face first in a pig's trough, wondering what went wrong. He musters up the courage to go home, hoping to be a servant in his father's house. He was met by a warm embrace and a celebration of welcoming.

Meanwhile, the older son grew bitter and jealous over how his father treated his younger son. He could not understand the reason to celebrate his return. He found no joy in it because his jealousy had stolen that joy. Be careful that your jealousy does not steal your joy as well.

When have you struggled to be glad for someone when something good happens to them?

Jealous of Evil

"Fret not yourself because of evildoers; be not envious of wrongdoers!" - Psalm 37:1

Have you ever been jealous of a wrongdoer? You probably can't think of a time that you can. Let me phrase the question in another way. Have you ever been tempted to cheat because you see others getting away with it? Have you ever been frustrated to see the bad guy win and the good guy lose? In those moments, you may be feeling jealousy over a 'wrongdoer'?

As you grow older, you'll notice more and more that life is not fair. The evil will seem to prosper more than the good. You'll be tempted to change your ways or at least wish you could. The palmist says to fret, not the evildoer. Filter those thoughts of jealousy with the thoughts of eternity. Our God will bring all things to right standing. While evil may prosper now, they will account for what they have done in the end.

How does God's ultimate justice change how you view others now?

I AM an Influencer

An Example

"Let no one despise you for your youth, but set the believers an example" - 1 Timothy 4:12

Timothy is a young pastor who is being trained and encouraged by Paul. In his letter to Timothy, he encourages the young man to be an example to all of the believers. Both young and old, Timothy was to be an influencer in their lives for the sake of holiness. This isn't just a command for pastors but for all believers to follow. We are all influencing someone, even if we're not intentional about it.

Over the following few devotions, we will think through what it means to be an influencer. For today, I want you to take time and think about whom you can influence. I don't mean on social media but in real life. What friend do you have that you can lead towards a better relationship with God?

Whom can you be influencing?

I AM an Influencer

In Speech

"in speech" - 1 Timothy 4:12

The first area that Paul tells Timothy to be an example in is in his speech. What does that mean? Indeed, Paul is not asking him to be an English teacher or a speech therapist. So, what is Paul after? He wants Timothy to set an example in his speech that showcases a sacred heart as Jesus taught about this in His ministry. The overflow of our hearts is what comes out of our mouths.

So, when Timothy is at the grocery store or playing a game with his friends, his speech should be seasoned with love, mercy, and godliness. When he loses the game, his speech isn't hateful or curt. When he has to wait in line, he isn't mumbling impatiently. We, too, need to set an example in our speech.

When do you struggle to have godly speech?

I AM an Influencer

In Conduct

"in conduct" - 1 Timothy 4:12

Practice what you preach. That's a saying that has been around for a long time, and you may be familiar with it. This is essentially Paul's subsequent encouragement to Timothy. Not only set an example in your speech but your conduct as well. What good would it do for Timothy to talk about holy things and encourage his brothers and sisters in Christ to follow Him if he himself did not act like a Christian?

This should be a constant test we ask ourselves. Are our actions and our words lining up? Hypocrisy has an incredibly damaging effect on our witness. If we want to share the Gospel and encourage other Christians in their faith, we have to practice what we preach.

In what area do you struggle to practice what you preach?

I AM an Influencer

In Love

"in love" - 1 Timothy 4:12

Here Paul gets to the root of the matter. What we say and what we do must be rooted in love. There are a bunch of possible motivations for what we do. We may encourage someone in order to manipulate them and convince them to join 'our side' of an argument. We may call someone to repent in front of others in order to humiliate them. We may share the Gospel with someone just to win an argument about faith.

When we have these motivations, I pray that the Holy Spirit would convict us quickly and sharply. It should be our love for God and our love for other people that drive us to action. It should inform everything that we do. Like the love for basketball drove Michael Jordan, the love for Jesus should drive our lives.

What other motivations have gotten in the way of loving someone?

I AM an Influencer

In Faith

"in faith" - 1 Timothy 4:12

How can we be an example in faith? There are ways to make your faith known on a daily basis, among others. You can talk about spiritual things with them. You can ask them if there is anything that you can pray for them about. You can talk about what you learned or experienced at church. Even your speech and conduct will be a sign of the faith that undergirds them.

However, the most illuminating way to display your faith is in the midst of trials. When your world is shaken, but your faith is not is when it will be most evident. So, I encourage you to do the work of strengthening your faith in the good days. This will prepare it to be on display in the difficult days to come.

What has shaken your faith before?

I AM an Influencer

In Purity

"in purity" - 1 Timothy 4:12

This is the last one on Paul's list to Timothy, and it could be assumed in the conduct or the motivation portion. However, Paul makes sure to include purity in this list. Why? Why is purity so crucial for Timothy to live an exemplary life? Timothy's purity not only affects his soul but the souls of everyone in his congregation. Whether or not he seeks purity will make a massive difference in the lives of the people that he leads and influences.

While you're not a pastor, you have a circle of influence. You have friends, family, classmates, and maybe even co-workers. If they know you're a Christian, they are looking to you to find out what it means to be a Christian. Set the example.

Why is purity essential?

I AM an Influencer

Follow Me

"Be imitators of me, as I am of Christ." - 1 Corinthians 11:1

Maybe you're like me, and you're struggling in this section. Maybe you're asking yourself, "What gives me the right to say, 'Follow me?'" If you're feeling inadequate and ill-equipped, I want to commend those feelings and redirect them. I want you to embrace your inadequacy because you are. We all are.

However, our story doesn't end with inability. It ends with Jesus doing the work we can't do. You see, it's not really us that we're asking others to follow. We're asking others to follow Jesus like we follow Jesus. This means that we won't do it perfectly, but we're following the Perfect One.

How does "as I am of Christ" change your perspective on being an influencer?

I AM an Influencer

Model Good Works

"Show yourself in all respects to be a model of good works, and in your teaching show integrity, dignity" - Titus 2:7

Take some time today to think about how you can be a model of good works. I'm not talking about big gestures like going to help at a soup kitchen or a homeless shelter. I think those are great, but I'm thinking more about the daily gestures that display kindness. What can you do each day to be a good model?

Here are a few suggestions you can think about. You can sit with someone at lunch who is eating alone. You can help someone with their homework or notes in class. You can pick up someone else's trash, so the janitor doesn't have to do it. You can ask each of your teachers if there is a way you can help them that day. Be creative and do good things.

Why is it important to model good works?

I AM an Influencer

Christ Is Our Influencer

"For I have given you an example, that you also should do just as I have done to you." - John 13:15

There are two overarching reasons why we are trying to be influencers. The first is that Jesus is our influencer, and the second is that we're seeking to have a Gospel influence on others. Let's talk about the first reason in this devotional today.

Jesus lived a perfect life. This truth can be forgotten when we think about His death and miraculous resurrection. However, His perfect life is not only our example to follow, but the basis for a death that was sacrificial. For His death to accomplish what it did, He has to have lived a holy life, without spot or blemish. Because He did, He secured our salvation and the power necessary for us to follow Him.

What is the significance of Jesus' perfect life?

I AM an Influencer

Gospel Influence

*"Keep your conduct among the Gentiles honorable
so that when they speak against you as evildoers,
they may see your good deeds and glorify God
on the day of visitation." - 1 Peter 2:12*

Here is the second goal of our desire to be influencers: that our lives will be a display of the Gospel. We won't be able to share the Gospel with everyone that we come in contact with. At least, we won't be able to do that in an effective way. What we can do is live a life that is exemplary of the Gospel in front of everyone and have those intentional conversations as often as we can.

Take inventory of your life and your actions today. Can you say that your life is exemplary of the Gospel? Or do you live a life so similar to those around you that they would never know that you're a believer? I encourage you, brother, to keep your conduct among non-Christians honorable for the sake of the Gospel.

How are you living a life that is exemplary of the Gospel?

I AM a Student

Work Hard

"Whatever you do, work heartily, as for the Lord and not for men," - Colossians 3:23

What does it mean to be a good or godly student? Over the next few devotionals, we will dive into that question. We will search what the Bible has to say about studying, work ethic, respect for your teachers, and the temptation to cheat.

The verse for today lays the foundation for all that we are going to talk about. It says that whatever we do, including being a student, we should do it for the Lord and not for men. This doesn't mean that we don't do it for men at all. We have teachers and parents that are involved, but the ultimate purpose is for our Lord.

Why do you forget that you're doing things for Jesus as well as others?

I AM a Student

Study Well

"Give instruction to a wise man, and he will be still wiser; teach a righteous man, and he will increase in learning." - Proverbs 9:9

There is no ceiling to what you can learn. There is always more to learn and more ways in which you can grow. Don't settle for a limited amount of training or knowledge in an area that you're passionate about. You can always do better and be better. Wise men can be wiser.

Let this be an encouragement to you if you struggle in your studies. The struggle means that you're a wise man getting wiser. It means that you haven't stopped growing. It means that you're still pursuing more extensive and better things for yourself. So struggle through, and by God's grace, you'll make it to the other side.

Where do you struggle to grow?

I AM a Student

Grow

"But grow in the grace and knowledge of our Lord and Savior Jesus Christ. To him be the glory both now and to the day of eternity. Amen."- 2 Peter 3:18

We're not only to grow generally, as we talked about in the last devotion. But we are to grow specifically in the grace and knowledge of Jesus. This means that we have to invest time into studying His word. We have to consider who He is and learn from Him.

This can be done in a bunch of different ways. You can read one chapter of the Bible a day and seek to understand it. You can listen and take notes to the sermon on Sunday. You can read a good book that talks about Jesus. You can listen to a podcast that is about spiritual things. Whatever you do, grow in the grace and knowledge of our Lord.

Why do people stop growing?

I AM a Student

Respect Teachers

"Let every person be subject to the governing authorities. For there is no authority except from God, and those that exist have been instituted by God." - Romans 13:1

When you're in a class with a teacher that you don't like, you'll be tempted to be disrespectful or dismissive of them. Romans 13:1 gives a far-reaching command to call Christians. We are to be submissive to the different authorities in our lives. This includes our school teachers. We should be respectful, even if we disagree with the teaching or how they go about teaching.

Why is this command given? Because all of our authorities in our lives are ultimately there at God's sovereign will. He placed those teachers in your life for a reason. He may not approve of their actions either, but He has called you to be submissive and respectful to them while you're in that class.

Do you have a teacher that you struggle to respect?

I AM a Student

Temptation to Cheat

"Better is a poor person who walks in his integrity than one who is crooked in speech and is a fool." - Proverbs 19:1

School can be tricky. Some of you may really struggle with all of the different classes that you have to take. At times it may feel like it is all too much to handle. A natural response to the pressures of school is to look for a shortcut or a way to make things simpler. When you reach that point, you'll be tempted to cheat.

Proverbs makes it clear that it is far better to struggle in your classes with integrity than to cheat your way to the top and lose any credibility. Someone who cheats thinks they are clever in the moment, but they are actually fools and crooked. Fight that temptation to take the easy way and press on towards integrity.

Why are you tempted to cheat?

I AM a Student

Damage of Cheating

"Lying lips are an abomination to the Lord, but those who act faithfully are his delight." - Proverbs 12:22

Cheating is foolish for a lot of reasons. One of those is that it is an abomination to your Lord. Why would you purposefully offend your God? The second is that cheating doesn't actually help you. Think about it. If you cheat your way to the top, eventually, there is no one else to cheat from, and you'll be found out.

When that happens, the fall is tremendously painful. Just like if you were to fall from the top of a tree or a tower, the higher you go, the more danger you're in. The longer you cheat and the higher you climb, the more detriment you'll endure in the end. Be faithful in your work and delight your God.

Why is cheating like lying?

I AM a Student

Increased Wisdom

*"And Jesus increased in wisdom and in stature
and in favor with God and man." - Luke 2:52*

This verse should be an encouragement to us all. Jesus had to study. He had to grow in wisdom and in stature before God and man. This is a mind-boggling truth if you think about it. Jesus is God. He has all knowledge and cannot learn anything because it's all already there. At the same time, Jesus is fully man. This means that He had some capacity to learn and grow.

Part of the answer to this wondrous mystery is in that Jesus emptied Himself of some of the rights He had as God in order to experience the life of a man in the fullest sense. God is not unfamiliar with your struggles in growth. He knows what it is like to sit in a school setting and have to learn. He experienced it and gives grace to you today to continue to work.

What encourages you about Jesus' humanity and divinity?

I AM a Student

Teachers Care

*"I will instruct you and teach you in the way you should go;
I will counsel you with my eye upon you." - Psalm 32:8*

Your teachers care about you. I know that there are bad apples in every bunch, and you may have a teacher who is really rough on their students. However, more times than not, your teachers deploy care for their students. Notice the final phrase in this proverb. It's a promise not only to teach but to be watchful over you.

They are watching to see you grow and to see where they can help in your struggle. Their primary goal is not to see good grades but to see progress and growth in your life. As a teacher of God's word, trust me when I say that your teachers care. Take time to thank a teacher today.

Who has been your favorite teacher, and why?

I AM a Student

Put It into Practice

"What you have learned and received and heard and seen in me—practice these things, and the God of peace will be with you." - Philippians 4:9

Practice what you've learned. The word "practice" has two important implications. The first is that you must act on what you've learned. The second is that you're not going to do it perfectly every time. If you've been watching a game film for a week before the football game, but you're unwilling to practice what you've seen, what good is that?

Take what you are learning and put it to good use. Whether you're learning grammar, athletic drills, or Bible study methods, don't let that knowledge go to waste. Practice it. Practice it to the point that you're able to teach someone based on your own learning and experience. This is how you make disciples.

What have you been neglecting to practice?

Fear of the Lord

"The fear of the Lord is the beginning of knowledge;
fools despise wisdom and instruction. – Proverbs" 1:7

Why is the beginning of knowledge the fear of the Lord? The answer is simple. All truth must come from somewhere or someone. The Bible teaches that God is the origin of all things, including what is genuine and not true. So, if you're going to have proper knowledge of anything, it has to begin with knowing who God is.

This is why your faith is not something you can put into a box and use only on Sundays or special occasions. It permeates every aspect of your life. As you learn math or science, you're learning the truth of God. So, embrace and rejoice in all truth, for it is all God's truth.

What do you think about the phrase,
"All truth is God's truth."?

I AM a Teammate

Play Your Part

"If the foot should say, "Because I am not a hand, I do not belong to the body," that would not make it any less a part of the body." - 1 Corinthians 12:15

In this letter to the Corinthian church, Paul uses a beautiful analogy to help us understand what the church is like. He describes it as the human body. It is made up of all different body parts. Each one has a different function that contributes to the whole. This makes the church a team of individuals with different skills, all working towards the same goal.

In your life, you're going to be in various teams. When you find yourself on a team, your goal is to play your part. Whether that means being the foot of the team or the hand, play your part. Whether goalie or striker, it is essential to know what role you're supposed to be playing.

What role are you best in on a team?

I AM a Teammate

Bigger Than You

"To each is given the manifestation of the Spirit for the common good." - 1 Corinthians 12:7

It can be easy to focus on ourselves when a part of a team. We can be brought down low by our own failures or get too caught up in our own successes. While your personal progress in the team is important, the more important thing is the team as a whole. Think about the game of football. On a play that scores, most of the players hit or get hit. Only one will make it into the endzone with the ball in hand.

The team you're on is more significant than yourself. It's not about you or about some star play. It is about the team and the team's mission on the field. Take time to look at the bigger picture and ask yourself what you can do for the team.

What would make you a better teammate?

I AM a Teammate

Help the Weak

"that there may be no division in the body, but that the members may have the same care for one another." - 1 Corinthians 12:25

There are some people on your teams who are going to be weaker than you and some that are going to be stronger. If you're on a robotics team, someone may have a great engineering mind but poor social skills. So, while they have good ideas, they may not know how to express them. Help those who are weaker in areas where you are strong.

When we support one another, we grow stronger together? This eliminates the division between weak and strong. It says to the whole team, we are all weak, and we are all strong in different ways. When the team works together, the whole team becomes strong. Look for those whom you can help grow.

What is an area in which you are strong?

I AM a Teammate

Step Out

"If the whole body were an eye, where would be the sense of hearing? If the whole body were an ear, where would be the sense of smell?" - 1 Corinthians 12:17

There will be a temptation, as you work on a team, to desire another person's position. Maybe you wish that you were the leader of the team. Or maybe the opposite is true. Maybe you're feeling the pressures of leadership and want to give that responsibility away. Whatever the case may be, there will be moments when you will envy someone else's position or abilities.

When those moments come, remember this verse. The whole body is not a collection of ears. That would be ridiculous, and it would not survive. The same is true of your team. Praise God for all of the parts of your team because everyone holds a vital place.

What teammate do you envy? Why?

I AM a Teammate

Step Up

"and on those parts of the body that we think less honorable we bestow the greater honor, and our unpresentable parts are treated with greater modesty" - 1 Corinthians 12:23

This is a complex topic to write about because it can be read in the wrong tone. The "less honorable" members of the team that Paul is referring to are not those who are worth less than others. He is not saying that they are dishonorable. He is talking about those members that are out of the spotlight. On the human body, this may be your pinky toe. No one really notices it, but it plays an important role.

Paul here is encouraging them to remember that the "less honorable" are worthy of honor. He would even argue that they might be worthy of more incredible honor because they do their job without thanks and without any glory.

Do you feel like a less honorable member of your team?

I AM a Teammate

Iron Sharpens Iron

"Iron sharpens iron, and one man sharpens another." - Proverbs 27:17

In this proverb, we are given one of the best word pictures about being on a team that there is. Simply said, "Iron sharpens iron." The reason this is true is because the metals are of the same hardness. If it were iron and butter, neither would be sharpened. Or even iron and aluminum. The aluminum would be sharpened but not the iron because it's softer.

Your brothers and sisters in Christ are made out of the same stuff you are. They have been bought by the blood of Jesus and saved by His grace. So rub shoulders with them. Learn from them. Let them sharpen you, and you sharpen them.

Whom can you sharpen this week?

I AM a Teammate

No Division

"I appeal to you, brothers, by the name of our Lord Jesus Christ, that all of you agree, and that there be no divisions among you, but that you be united in the same mind and the same judgment." - 1 Corinthians 1:10

Therein lies the key to success for any team: unity. Jesus said that a house divided against itself could not stand. It is imperative that the team be of the same mind and the same judgment. However, this seems impossible to find. Teams are made up of different people with different ideas and experiences. Naturally, there is going to be conflict and division.

What do you do when that arises? When the team is divided, there must be a more remarkable thing that unites them. For the Christian in the church setting, it is our mutual salvation and love for Jesus. For the soccer team, it is the mutual desire to win and love for the game. When you come up against conflict, look for that common ground to unite around.

What is the last conflict you had with a teammate?

I AM a Teammate

Get Advice

"Where there is no guidance, a people fall, but in an abundance of counselors there is safety." - Proverbs 11:14

This verse has become more and more important to me as I've gotten older. I wish I would have taken it to heart years ago when I was a teenager. I'm not experiencing a lot of new things happening. I'm starting a new job, buying a home for the first time, and moving to a new area. I would be lost if it were not for the abundance of counselors that I've sought out.

You, too, have a lot going on in your life. Soon, you will have to make decisions about what college to go to or what field or work to begin in. You'll start at your first job and be on your way to moving out of your parents' house. Start asking for advice today. Not just in the big things, but in the little things as well.

Who can you go to for advice?

I AM a Teammate

God's Workers, Field, and Building

"For we are God's fellow workers. You are God's field, God's building." - 1 Corinthians 3:9

In this verse, Paul gives three illustrations of what kind of team you're on. As a Christian, you are a part of the body of Christ. You're united with the local church and the universal church in different ways. Let's take a moment to unpack these three ideas.

The first is that we are fellow workers. We are made to be involved in His work. We are also God's field. We are a place to grow and bring a harvest. Finally, we are God's building. We are a place for Him to dwell. When God dwells in us, we grow and go to work.

How does God dwelling in you change your team dynamic?

I AM a Teammate

Serve the Team

"As each has received a gift, use it to serve one another, as good stewards of God's varied grace:" - 1 Peter 4:10

When you're saved, God will show you what kind of gifts He has given you. Some of you will be natural teachers, and some will be very welcoming to new friends. Others will be good listeners, while others will have deep compassion for people across the world. Whatever those gifts are, use them to serve your team at the local church.

Some of those gifts will need to be developed, so don't be discouraged if you can't do what you want on day one. Ask someone to help you grow in the area that you're gifted in and get to work serving in the best way that you can.

What is one of your gifts?

I AM Single

It's Good to Be Single

"I want you to be free from anxieties. The unmarried man is anxious about the things of the Lord, how to please the Lord." - 1 Corinthians 7:32

If you're single and hating it, this may be one of the most discouraging verses that you read today. What I want to do, as we start this new section of devotionals, is to highlight the encouragement to find in being single.

The first thing to see is that the single person is free from anxieties that come from a committed relationship with a woman. Whether married or just dating, those kinds of relationships add complexities to your life. So, while you're single, embrace and enjoy the lack of anxieties and use your extra time for the Lord.

How do you feel about your singleness?

Don't Make Yourself Fall

"I adjure you, O daughters of Jerusalem, by the gazelles or the does of the field, that you not stir up or awaken love until it pleases." - Song of Solomon 3:5

One of the hardest temptations you will face while being single is lust. The way the Song of Solomon phrases it is that we should not stir up or awaken love until it pleases. This means that as we think about being in a relationship with someone or grow in our envy of other couples, we stir up what should be love.

Instead, what we're stirring up is jealousy and hurt feelings. Wait for the Lord. Wait for Him to give to you the person that He has for you. If you are patient until that time, you will find that the love stirred up between you and that person is far greater than anything you could have formed in your own mind.

Why do you struggle with being jealous of other relationships?

Delight in The Lord

"Delight yourself in the Lord, and he will give you the desires of your heart." - Psalm 37:4

While you're waiting for the Lord to provide that person for you, delight in the Lord, the best way to fight against temptation is to replace it with greater love. More than you love the idea of being with someone, love Jesus. Delight in Him. Take pleasure in your relationship with Him first and foremost.

After you have delighted in the Lord, notice the promise. For those who delight in the Lord, He will give them the desires of their heart. Most importantly, He will give you Himself because you will delight in Him supremely. Along with that, at the right time, God will give you the spouse you've been waiting for. So, delight in Him.

How can you delight in God?

I AM Single

Better to Be Alone

"It is better to live in a desert land than with a quarrelsome and fretful woman." - Proverbs 21:19

Singleness can lead to loneliness. When you're lonely, you'll be tempted to rush into a relationship just so you won't be alone. I want to strongly warn you against this. Both form personal experience and from Scripture. Let me say it's better to be alone than with the wrong person.

The way the proverb makes it humorous. It's better to live in a desert than with the wrong woman. Once the laughing ceases, you'll realize the devastating truth here. It's better to be stranded and miserable than stuck with the wrong person. Trust that God's plan for your life is for your good and His glory?

What are the dangers of being with the wrong person?

If You Love It, Let It Go

"For whoever would save his life will lose it, but whoever loses his life for my sake will find it. – Matthew" 16:25

The essence of following Jesus is giving up everything for Him. However, the nature of our God is not just to take from His people. He takes from them and gives back a better version of what they had. Like a father who takes a deflated kickball from his child to replace it with a new one, He is working for our good.

Here's my challenge for you today. Give your love life to Jesus. Trust Him with it. Stop striving so hard after it and wringing your hands over whom you want to be with. If you're really struggling in this area, begin each day with a simple prayer. Confess to Him your struggle and your desire to trust Him.

How does giving Jesus your love life help you?

I AM Single

Grow While You Wait

*"But as for you, O man of God, flee these things.
Pursue righteousness, godliness, faith, love,
steadfastness, gentleness." - 1 Timothy 6:11*

Implicit in most singleness conversations is a long period of waiting. Rarely does someone meet their spouse at a young age. This means that you probably have years of waiting ahead of you. So, here's what you need to be doing while you wait: grow.

Grow into what you want to be when you find your wife. Don't wait until you find someone to start getting yourself together. Don't wait until you're in the midst of a relationship to start thinking about what you need to do when you're in a relationship. Start preparing your heart now for what it needs to be then.

*What kind of person do you want
to be when you meet your wife?*

I AM Single

God's Heart for Singles

"To the eunuchs who keep my Sabbaths, who choose the things that please me and hold fast my covenant, I will give in my house and within my walls a monument and a name better than sons and daughters; I will give them an everlasting name that shall not be cut off." - Isaiah 56:5-4

If you're a struggling single, I want you to read this verse and hold onto it. God loves you. He loves you deeply, and He has not forgotten you. Because of their physical disability, eunuchs were outcasts in society and often lived their entire lives in singleness. God makes an incredible promise to these people.

He promises a place of belonging, a family to be a part of, and a name to be known by. God knows your struggle. He sees you and what you're going through. He cares. He has an excellent plan for you and promises made to you.

What fears are calmed with these promises?

If You Can't Keep from Lusting

"But if they cannot exercise self-control, they should marry. For it is better to marry than to burn with passion." - 1 Corinthians 7:9

Paul does encourage anyone who can be single to remain single. However, Paul knew that most men did not choose to be single. In fact, most men would choose to be in a relationship today if they could. So, recognizing this, Paul says, if you cannot control your lust, you should marry.

This doesn't mean you should marry the first person that says yes. It does mean that you have full liberty to pursue a relationship with the ultimate goal of finding a spouse. God does not desire to torture you but to nurture you until you're ready to find that person. So be on the lookout and be ready to pursue her when the time comes.

What are you looking for in a partner?

It's Not Good to Be Alone

"Then the Lord God said, "It is not good that the man should be alone; I will make him a helper fit for him." - Genesis 2:18

Following such a section on singleness, I want to address dating from a biblical perspective. Before we can begin, we must acknowledge that dating is not found in the Bible. At that time in history, dating wasn't really a thing that people did. This does not mean that dating is wrong or sinful. It does mean that we have to look for principles from the Bible as opposed to specific verses when we think about dating.

The first verse to consider is the design of God. God did not design us to live alone. He designed us for a relationship. Specifically, he designed men to be in relationships in a unique way that cannot be fulfilled with the same gender. In God's perfect design, there is a relationship. That's why you have such a desire to be in a relationship.

What is your current dating relationship like?

I AM Dating

As Christ Loved the Church

"Husbands, love your wives, as Christ loved the church and gave himself up for her" - Ephesians 5:25

Most of what the Bible has to say about dating comes from the lens of marriage. I would argue that that's the very point of dating. If you begin dating someone and realize that you would never marry them, then you should end that relationship because you'll be wasting time and your partner's time.

Here the command is to love your wife sacrificially. For a dating relationship, the principle is the same. We should care for our partners sacrificially, putting their needs and wants before our own. There is a line not to be crossed here because you aren't married, but generally, sacrifice what it takes to care for your partner well.

What sacrifices might you have to make when dating?

Purify Her

"that he might sanctify her, having cleansed her by the washing of water with the word" - Ephesians 5:26

Let's be very clear at the beginning of this devotion. You cannot purify your partner. It is the word of God that does the work. You're not on a holy high horse able to call her sin out and make her into a better person. Both of you are fully dependent on the grace of God for growth.

However, it is the unique responsibility of the man in the relationship to lead the charge towards holiness. Whomever you begin dating, lead her towards Jesus. This can look like regularly praying together or sharing what you're learning about in the Bible. You don't have to teach her, and you shouldn't preach at her. But you should lovingly lead her closer to Jesus.

How can you lead your partner closer to Jesus?

Boaz Protected

"Have I not charged the young men not to touch you? And when you are thirsty, go to the vessels and drink what the young men have drawn." - Ruth 2:9

A great place to look for lessons on how to treat a woman is the book of Ruth. It is one of the greatest love stories in the Bible and arguably of all time. Without getting into too many details, Ruth was a refugee who found herself in Boaz's field picking up leftover grain. She did this to provide for herself and her mother-in-law. When Boaz saw her, he was smitten and sought to protect her.

That's one of your jobs in your relationships. Protect your partner not only from physical harm but from spiritual and emotional as well. Be a safe place for her to find herself and a safe person for her to be around.

Why is it your job to protect your partner?

I AM Dating

Boaz Pursued

"Then Boaz said to his young man who was in charge of the reapers, "Whose young woman is this?" - Ruth 2:5

Here is the key to a healthy dating relationship. Pursue the girl. When Boaz saw her and found her attractive, he pursued her. He built a relationship of trust and friendship, which blossomed ultimately into a marriage.

Take the first step. Initiate the conversation. Fight the fear that might be holding you back and begin that relationship with the girl that you like. If you're in a relationship, don't stop pursuing her. Keep getting to know her better. Keep finding ways to love her and care for her. Once you start, never stop dating.

How can you pursue your partner this week?

Love Is the Foundation

*"Love is patient and kind; love does not envy or boast;
it is not arrogant" - 1 Corinthians 13:4*

The foundation of any dating relationship is love. In order to have a good idea of what biblical love is, let's take a few devotions to discuss 1 Corinthians 13. This has been called the love chapter because it contains a thorough and beautiful definition of love. If you have been to a wedding, you've probably heard these verses read while you were there.

Love is patient and kind; love does not envy or boast; it is not arrogant. We are often not very loving to our partners. When we lack patience, we lack love. When we are arrogant and prideful, we are not being loved. All these other sinful attitudes don't end at themselves. They ultimately reveal a lack of love in that moment.

How has this verse changed your perspective on love?

Love Is Not Rude

"or rude. It does not insist on its own way; it is not irritable or resentful" - 1 Corinthians 13:5

Love is not rude. It does not insist on its own way; it is not irritable or resentful. I'm writing these verses in the devotions again, so you're forced to slow down and really read them. Ponder this one for a moment and think to yourself. Have you been irritable or resentful lately? Have you been demanding of your own way?

These are such natural areas to fall short. This is why we so desperately need the love of Jesus. Not only to save us from the punishment we incur while sinning in these ways but also to help us to love our partners better. Lean into the love of Jesus as you strive to love your partner well this week.

How have you been demanding this week?

I AM Dating

Love Is Truth

"it does not rejoice at wrongdoing but rejoices with the truth." - 1 Corinthians 13:6

Love does not rejoice at wrongdoing but rejoices with the truth. Love finds its joy in the truth. When we spend our time trying to manipulate or deceive our partners, we are spending time not loving them. Be truthful and honest with your partner if you want to show them, love.

This means that you shouldn't be afraid if she decides to pick up your phone and look through it. You should have nothing to hide when you're having a conversation about her, and she walks up. But truthful with her and, in so doing, love her.

When have you tried to hide something from your partner?

Strength in Love

"Love bears all things, believes all things, hopes all things, endures all things." - 1 Corinthians 13:7

This is my favorite section of the definition. Love bears all things, believes all things, hopes all things, endures all things. This section describes the incredible strength of love. At the end of the day, we are all going to fail at loving our partners perfectly. This is why strength has to be baked into love.

Love assumes the best and forgives the worst in our partners. Hold onto this verse when you've messed up tremendously and let this verse sober you when you've been hurt by your partner. Choose to love first.

Why is strength important in love?

I AM Dating

Sexual Purity

"Let marriage be held in honor among all, and let the marriage bed be undefiled, for God will judge the sexually immoral and adulterous." - Hebrews 13:4

Sex is designed for marriage. Not for a dating relationship or two people who love each other. It is designed to be enjoyed by a man and a woman in a marriage relationship. This is the best way for it to be enjoyed because there is deep and lasting trust and commitment. These boundaries don't hinder joy but enhance it.

So fight for sexual purity in your relationships. This means that you draw the line and make sure things don't go too far. This means that you don't wander into lust or stray towards watching pornography. Fight for sexual purity now and reap the rewards on that day when you're married.

Why is sexual purity important for your soul?

Wife Is a Favor from God

"He who finds a wife finds a good thing and obtains
favor from the Lord." - Proverbs 18:22

A wife is a gift from God. You don't deserve a partner, but God, in His kindness, will choose to give you one day. Don't mistake that gift for a right. Don't that her for granted as if you earned her or have purchased her in some way. God gave you to each other to be enjoyed and sanctified by each other.

Take a moment now to praise God for the great gift that is coming your way. Praise Him that one day He will give you the perfect person to walk through this life with. Ask Him to show you who that is and give you patience in the meantime.

What is your perfect person like?

I AM Dating

Proverbs 31 Woman - Compassion

"She opens her hand to the poor and reaches out her hands to the needy." - Proverbs 31:20

If you're not sure what you should be looking for in a wife, consider Proverbs 31. It is an incredible description that would bless any husband. Let's use our last two devotions in this section to think about what a Proverbs 31 woman is like.

In this verse, she is described as someone full of compassion for those in need. She doesn't just open her hand to those in her home, but those without a home. Simply put, she cares about other people. Let that be on the top of your list of qualities for what you're looking for in a wife.

Why is compassion so important to find in a partner?

I AM Dating

Proverbs 31 Woman - Balance

"Strength and dignity are her clothing, and she laughs at the time to come." - Proverbs 31:25

Here we find three things put into balance: strength, dignity, and laughter. The Proverbs 31 woman knows when to be strong. She knows how to stand up for herself and for others. She also knows when to be dignified. She understands that there are times to be reverent and respectful to the people she is around. Finally, she knows when to laugh. She is a balanced woman.

Try this different prayer for your future spouse. Pray that she is balanced. Pray that you can have fun with her as well as be serious with her. Pray that you can trust her to have your back as much as you can trust her to pull a prank on you. Pray that she is balanced.

Why is balance so important in a relationship?

I AM Different

Different Walk

"I, therefore, a prisoner for the Lord, urge you to walk in a manner worthy of the calling to which you have been called" - Ephesians 4:1

This was a hard fact for me to swallow when I was a teenager. I want to fit in so much that I couldn't accept the fact that I'm different. The ironic thing is that everyone is different. It's the only thing that we all truly have in common. Over these last few devotions, let's embrace these differences

The first is that we have a different walk. We simply live our lives differently from those around us. We seek to walk in a way that honors God in all we do. We make our decisions, and even our friends, with this lens.

How do you feel about being different?

I AM Different

Different Talk

"If anyone thinks he is religious and does not bridle his tongue but deceives his heart, this person's religion is worthless." - James 1:26

We have a different walk and a different talk. What we talk about, how we talk about them, and the reason we talk about those things are all affected by our love for Jesus. This means that we talk about godly things and things that are of common grace (weather, sports, TV, etc.). This also means that we talk without unbridled anger or manipulation.

This finally means that we talk about these things and these people with pure motivations. Gossip is talking about someone in order to damage them or their reputation in the sight of others. When we talk about others, let it be to lift them up or bring up real concerns to those who can help.

Why is it hard to tame your tongue, as James writes about?

I AM Different

Different Goals

"But you will receive power when the Holy Spirit has come upon you, and you will be my witnesses in Jerusalem and in all Judea and Samaria, and to the end of the earth." - Acts 1:8

This gets at the foundation of our differences between the average person and us. If you're a Christian, you've been commissioned. Jesus has given you marching orders, and you have different goals from your non-believing friends. Our mission and our goal in life is to be a witness to the Gospel of Jesus Christ.

Are you living in a way that accomplishes this mission? Is this your goal when you wake up in the morning? Embrace this difference you have with the world because it displays a life-saving and life-changing reality. Jesus loves the world so much that He died to save all who would believe in Him.

How are your goals different from that of your friends?

I AM Different

Different Thoughts

"Finally, brothers, whatever is true, whatever is honorable, whatever is just, whatever is pure, whatever is lovely, whatever is commendable, if there is any excellence, if there is anything worthy of praise, think about these things." - Philippians 4:8

Out of the overflow of the heart, the mouth speaks. For the Christian, we are encouraged to fill our minds and, ultimately, our hearts with whatever is good. Paul gives a full definition of what is good. He uses descriptors like pure, true, and honorable to give us categories of what to think about.

How can we keep our minds on things like that? The first way is to filter out the bad. Don't watch a television show that is filled with tempting things. Don't listen to music that is laced with foul language and ideas. Instead, replace those things with wholesome media. It doesn't have to be explicitly Christian. But it should be true, honorable, and just.

What media do you need to filter out?

I AM Different

Different Attitude

"Have this mind among yourselves, which is yours in Christ Jesus" - Philippians 2:5

Attitude makes a big difference. The way you approach a situation can make or break how something goes. The attitude that we are called to have is the same attitude of Jesus Christ. You can summarize this attitude in one word: humility.

Jesus humbled Himself and left the perfection of glory to be born as a baby in a stable. He humbled Himself and endured a life of rejection by those He came to save. He humbled Himself and subjected Himself to death on a cross. If this was the attitude of our Lord, let it be ours as well.

What can you begin to do to increase your humility?

I AM Different

Different Self-Esteem

"I have been crucified with Christ. It is no longer I who live, but Christ who lives in me. And the life I now live in the flesh I live by faith in the Son of God, who loved me and gave himself for me." - Galatians 2:20

Self-esteem is important. There is no denying that. However, there are two types of self-esteem. There is a type of self-esteem that comes from within. It is where you find all of your worth and value in yourself. You're dependent on yourself alone. The issue with that is that you're going to fail yourself and disappoint yourself.

The Bible teaches us to find our self-esteem in Christ. See not only what He has done to save you, but what He has said about you. He has said that you're of incredible value and worth in His eyes. He has said that He wants you to be a part of His family. He has said you play an integral role in the church. Have Christ-informed self-esteem.

How are those forms of self-esteem different?

151

I AM Different

Different God

"There is none holy like the Lord: for there is none besides you; there is no rock like our God." - 1 Samuel 2:2

I'm so thankful for this difference. We have a different God. He is One that stands alone and above any other false god or idol. There is genuinely no one like our God. There is no one who can be compared to Him. He is different and calls us to be different.

There is no other God as powerful that He can create all things out of nothing. There is no other God, so just that He will not let an ounce of sin go unpunished. There is no other God so merciful as to save the sinners from His own wrath by His own blood. Praise God that He is so different from the rest!

What is your favorite thing about God?

Different People

"But you are a chosen race, a royal priesthood, a holy nation, a people for his own possession, that you may proclaim the excellencies of him who called you out of darkness into his marvelous light." - 1 Peter 2:9

We are a part of different people. This is the beautiful paradox of Christianity. While we are called to be distinct and different from the world, we are not called to do this in isolation. We have a family of spiritual brothers and sisters that we can lean on and trust in. We have a local church that we can be a part of.

In all of these other areas of difference, we have a group of people that are like-minded with us. We can walk differently together. We can talk differently together. We can have the different goal of sharing the Gospel together. We may be different, but we are not alone.

How does being a part of a body of believers make you feel?

I AM Different

Different Privileges

"and if children, then heirs—heirs of God and fellow heirs with Christ, provided we suffer with him in order that we may also be glorified with him." - Romans 8:17

In our final devotion together, let's celebrate the different privileges we have as God's people. Let me remind you that you did not earn a single one of these things. You were not chosen because you were unique or talented in any way. You have been gifted these things by the grace of God. They are not to be lorded over others but treasured by us.

Now, let's rejoice. If we are in Christ, we are heirs with Christ. Think for a moment of all that belongs to Jesus. Everything. Literally everything. If we are followers of His, we are also heirs with Him. We will enjoy all things with Him. His joy will be our joy. What a privilege. What a future we have in store.

What do you think about this great privilege of those who believe in Jesus?

Conclusion

In Christ, we have an identity that cannot be shaken. Because Jesus is an all-powerful and abundantly gracious God, as long as we trust in Him, we have nothing to fear. This faith that is placed in our Lord affects every area of our lives. From being a student to being in a dating relationship, our commitment to follow Jesus will change how we are in these situations. This is a good thing. This means that we don't have to figure these things out on our own. This means that we don't have to try to be like someone else and fall short. It means that we have a Savior who not only gives us our identity but gives us the strength to be who we are. I pray that these devotions have helped you along the way as you are becoming who you are.